Answers for Emily

HALO Publications

1280 Armour Road
Bourbonnais, Illinois 60914

Copyright © 2018 by Joyce Anglea

ISBN # 978-0-9996667-0-8

First printing, 2018
Second printing, 2019

All scripture references are from the King James Bible.

All rights reserved. This book or any portion thereof may not be reproduced or used in any manner whatsoever without the express written permission of the publisher except for the use of brief quotations in a book review.

Printed in the United States of America

Answers for Emily

PRACTICAL ADVICE FOR CHRISTIAN WIVES AND MOTHERS

Mrs. Joyce Anglea

Dedication

This book is lovingly dedicated to Mrs. Emily Hanson and all of the other young women in the ministry who have asked me for advice. May God bless you as you strive to serve Him by serving your husbands and families in your respective ministries.

Acknowledgments

My heartfelt thanks are extended to the following people:

- My husband, Dr. Terry Anglea, for reading every answer and encouraging me to put them into print.
- Our six children, Hannah, Ben, Abbie, Luke, Leah, and Cherith, for the choices you have made which give credibility to this book.
- Linda Stubblefield for layout design and answering all of my many questions.
- Carrie Merriott for the beautiful cover design.
- Jessica Anglea, Naomi Bragg, and Sharon Thomason for their expertise in proofreading.

About the Author

Mrs. Joyce Anglea is the wife of Dr. Terry Anglea, the pastor of Faith Baptist Church in Bourbonnais, Illinois. While serving with her husband in full-time ministry, she has enjoyed singing in the choir, working in the church nursery, teaching Sunday school, giving devotionals at bridal and baby showers, and speaking to ladies at conferences and banquets. She is the mother of six children, all of whom are married, and along with their spouses are serving the Lord in their respective church ministries. Mrs. Anglea enjoys sewing, reading and spending time with her family.

Table of Contents

Foreword by Dr. Terry Anglea 13

Preface by Mrs. Emily Hanson 15

Introduction 17

Giving Attendance to Reading 19

My Wonderful Treasure. 29

As a Child 35

There Is a Season 47

Traditions 55

Never Enough Time. 67

An Help Meet for Him. 77

Feed Me, I'm Yours! 91

Boys Will Be Boys. 99

Sugar and Spice and Everything Nice 109

Readin' and 'Ritin' and 'Rithmetic 119

Every Wise Woman Buildeth Her House 127

Foreword
Dr. Terry Anglea

In June of 1979, God gave me a wonderful gift of His grace when He allowed me to marry Joyce Christner. She has truly been God's *"help meet"* for me.

I admire her more than words can express. I have lived with her for these many years and can truthfully say she is a great Christian. She is a wonderful wife. She is also a great mother and now grandmother, affectionately called *Mimi*. In addition to these, she is a tremendous ministry wife.

I know what you will read in this book are truths she has learned and lived. She speaks from what she has learned from her dad and mom growing up on an Iowa farm. She speaks from what she has learned from the Bible, reading it consistently and hearing it preached and taught. She has learned from some good books and from observation of the lives of others as well.

Most of what you read she has learned and lived from experience. She is gifted with one of God's rare blessings—common sense. I have listened as she explained how she came to conclusions concerning certain matters and marveled at the wisdom in her thinking. I trust what she has learned and lived will be a significant help to you.

If I sound like a biased, partisan husband— good—because I am, and I should be. May God bless you, the reader, as you learn from one of His choice servants.

Preface
Mrs. Emily Hanson

One way God shows us His amazing goodness is placing instrumental people in our lives *"for such a time as this."* Mrs. Joyce Anglea has been one such person in my life. God brought me under her direct influence when my husband and I were taking our first steps in the full-time ministry. She has been a godly example of how a Christian woman—ministry or non-ministry—should live. She has a plethora of wisdom for ladies who desire to be better Christians, wives, mothers, and keepers at home. Every lady—young or old—can learn from her. She has spent much time reading good material, seeking wisdom from godly sources, and applying that knowledge to her life. She has taken to heart what God instructed the "aged women" to do in Titus 2, that of teaching the young women.

This book is the culmination of a lifetime of gleaning, trial-and-error, and practice. Her walk with the Lord, manner of conduct, care for her family, and service in various church ministries has always intrigued me. She has an amazing balance of grace and spunk! I trust you will be as delighted, refreshed, and inspired reading her book as I was when I read it. This book is a must-have—one to be passed down from generation to generation. Thank the Lord for a godly woman who has dared to be transparent and teach us how to live the abundant Christian life…right.

Introduction

Several years ago, one of our young assistant pastor's wives, Emily Hanson, wrote me a letter asking for answers to twelve different questions. As I skimmed through these questions, my mind went back to when I, too, was a young assistant pastor's wife. I remembered having the same questions and searching for the answers. I also thought about other young women who had asked of me the same or similar questions. Then the words, "You should write a book," which I had heard many times in the last several years, came to mind. *Should I really attempt to write a book?* I wondered. I decided to go for it. So here we are with my *Answers for Emily* manuscript in hand. I hope it will be a help, blessing, and encouragement to any who read it.

#1

What books are on your recommended "Top 20" reading list?

"Till I come, give attendance to reading...."

– 1 Timothy 4:13

Giving Attendance to Reading

I love to read! My relationship with books began as a result of growing up in a home without a television. While other children spent their evenings watching *The Addams Family* or *The Brady Bunch*, I spent mine solving mysteries with Nancy Drew and her pals, Bess and George.

Once I outgrew Nancy Drew, I discovered the wonderful world of Grace Livingston Hill and Emily Loring. After that, I was hooked on books for life. Rare is the day I do not have a book close by that I am not reading.

Throughout my married life, I have enjoyed reading a variety of books. These are the top twenty that I would recommend:

Marriage

Woman the Completer by Dr. Jack Hyles

This book is a compilation of several sermons preached by Dr. Hyles at various Christian Womanhood Spectaculars. The sermon "Woman the Completer" is my favorite. I heard him preach it in person, bought it on tape, and was thrilled when I discovered it in print. It is a classic!

The Right Romance in Marriage by Dr. Cathy Rice
I was with my pastor's wife, Mrs. Dianne Brown, when she recommended this book to a young woman who was having trouble in her marriage. I read it out of curiosity. I am glad I did. The book was a great help in my early years of marriage.

The Proper Care and Feeding of Husbands
by Dr. Laura Schlessinger
One statement in this book alone was worth every minute it took to read it from beginning to end. (You'll have to read it yourself and guess which one!) I love her punchy, in-your-face approach.

Intended for Pleasure by Dr. Ed Wheat
This book will answer any technical questions you may have about intimacy.

Motherhood

How to Rear Infants by Dr. Jack Hyles
How to Rear Children by Dr. Jack Hyles

Giving Attendance to Reading

How to Rear Teenagers by Dr. Jack Hyles
We pretty much reared our six children according to the principles written in these three books.

Homemaking

With Love…and a Pinch of Salt by Jessie Rice Sandberg
Mrs. Sandberg wrote this book with her daughter's upcoming marriage in mind. It is full of bits of wisdom, articles, recipes, how-to's and so much more. It is a great reference book for homemaking.

Order in the Court by Sherry Hutson Camperson
An absolute must for common sense organization of the home.

Pastor's Wives

First We Have Coffee by Margaret Jensen
Mrs. Jensen grew up in an immigrant Norwegian pastor's home. This book, which is her mother's story, is written through the eyes of an adoring daughter.

Known Only to God by Martha Love
The author of this booklet shares her heart concerning

miscarriage. Because I have never experienced this sorrow, I have never been able to say, "I know how you feel" to someone who has. I keep several of these books on hand, so when someone I know has a miscarriage, I can give them one to let them know I care.

Through Gates of Splendor by Elisabeth Elliot
    The commitment and sacrifice displayed by these five missionary couples puts me to shame. This book challenges me to stay focused on what truly is important in this life.

Women (in General)

Lies Women Believe and the Truth That Sets Them Free by Nancy Leigh DeMoss
    When it comes to women, this author is certainly not ignorant of Satan's devices.

So Long, Insecurity by Beth Moore
    Most women struggle with insecurity—some more than others. Mrs. Moore explores the many reasons why and how to deal with each of them.

Changepoints by Joyce Landorf
    This book will help any woman accept gracefully the inevitable changes in her life.

Giving Attendance to Reading

Let Me Be a Woman by Elisabeth Elliot

Elisabeth Elliot wrote this book with the purpose of preparing her daughter for the changes that would take place in her life once she was married. She emphasizes the fact that men and women are created differently and the wife's responsibility to deal with those differences.

A Woman's World by Dr. Clyde Narramore

Dr. Narramore is a Christian psychologist from years gone by. In this book he addresses twelve problems that are common to women in general. It is a shame this book is out of print, as any woman would benefit from reading it.

Bible Topics

I Come Quietly to Meet You by Amy Carmichael

A book of thirty-one devotionals that are rich in spiritual nutrients. Reading one chapter in the morning is like starting your day with a breakfast of steak and eggs.

Biographies

Kitty, My Rib by E. Jane Mall

I read this book on Katherine Luther while in college. It was inspiring. Although tattered and torn, it is still in my library today.

Answers for Emily

Just for Fun

Love Comes Softly by Janette Oke

I love a good love story, and this is definitely one of the best. I have never read anything by Janette Oke that I did not like, but I have never read anything by her that I liked better than this one!

So there you have them—my "Top 20" suggestions for reading! Although I cannot endorse everything that is written in all of these books, there is a wealth of information in each one of them that has proven to be of value to me. While reading, I kept in mind that the authors may not be saved or may not be practicing their Christianity in accordance to the Biblical principles that I have been taught. I compared everything I read with what the Bible says and how it was preached to me.

Mason Cooley, an English professor from days gone by, said, "Reading gives us someplace to go when we have to stay where we are." As a young couple with only one car and a limited income, I spent the majority of my days at home with the children. While they were napping, I was reading. It gave me someplace to go when I had to stay where I was!

I understand that times have changed with the progression of the Internet. We have so much information available to us with the touch of a fingertip. I am glad we do. I do not know how we ever survived without our tablets and smart phones. But I am also glad that before they were invented, I was given the opportunity to read many good books. Doing so was definitely not a waste of time!

#2

What is your favorite way to read through your Bible in a year?

What method has helped you the most? Why?
What Bible study helps or methods do you use?
Which one(s) has helped you the most?

I have a wonderful treasure,
The gift of God without measure.
And so we travel together
My Bible and I!

My Wonderful Treasure

How many times did I spend the last day of December speed-reading through the entire book of Revelation? Too many to count for sure! All that effort was not because I wanted a certificate saying I had read my Bible through in a year's time. It was because I *did not* want to be embarrassed by not getting one for not doing so. However, it was because of these yearly programs that I was given a goal for my daily Bible-reading time. For that I am truly grateful. Although I had been reading my Bible on a somewhat consistent basis, it was not until this challenge was presented to me that I became totally committed. I owe a great big thank-you to Dr. Larry Brown, my pastor at Marion Avenue Baptist Church in Washington, Iowa, for setting me on the right course!

For my daily Bible reading, I use a daily Bible-reading schedule. These schedules are available from many different resources, and I like to keep several on hand. Some have one passage of Scripture to read per day, and others have two passages—one for the morning and one for the evening. I prefer the latter and read just one of the passages per day. This past January I found a chronological Bible-reading schedule online and decided to give it a try. I am enjoying it and thinking I might like to have a chronological Bible someday. Not sure…just thinking!

Along with the Bible-reading schedule, I read one page in the Psalms (for sweetness) and the chapter in Proverbs that corresponds with the day's date (for wisdom). If I am on a time restraint, I may only read the page in Psalms and/or the chapter in Proverbs.

Although I applaud anyone who reads the entire Bible through in a year's time, I prefer reading it in this manner. I get more enjoyment and find myself more attentive when I am not reading under pressure.

Concerning Bible Study

While at Marion Avenue I had the wonderful privilege of team-teaching the teenage girls Sunday School class with my pastor's wife, Mrs. Dianne Brown. I had taught elementary classes before but never high school girls. Every other week I had to prepare a lesson that involved more than telling a story from the Bible. I was forced to study. I started with the three books that were available to me at the time:

- *Strong's Exhaustive Concordance of the Bible*

My Wonderful Treasure

- *All the Men of the Bible* by Herbert Lockyear
- *All the Women of the Bible* by Herbert Lockyear

The *Strong's Concordance* was my husband's book that he was required to purchase while in Bible college. It is a huge book with very fine print. I used this book for looking up Scripture references as well as meanings of specific words. Now I use a computer program called PowerBible. (Isn't computer technology the best?)

It did not take long to figure out the easiest lessons to teach were lessons about people. No matter what passage of Scripture I was studying, I would pick out one or two characters from the passage and read what Mr. Lockyear had to say about them. From there I would list the lessons I could apply to my own heart and life. Then I would teach those lessons to the class. I am still using this method today.

Many times in my daily Bible reading I will come across the names of people that are intriguing to me, and I still go get my very tattered and worn copies of these books and stop to look them up. Agur, Jakeh, Ithiel and Ucal, mentioned in Proverbs 30:1, are my most recent lookups.

Bible reading is best done in the morning, but it does not hurt to have a backup plan just in case something goes haywire. (And how likely is it that something will go haywire? Very!) However, I strongly discourage married women from reading their Bibles in bed before going to bed with their husbands. A godly husband will want his wife to read her Bible, but I do not think he wants her to read it on his time!

For years I have pictured my Bible as:

- A love letter from God to me
- An instruction manual for getting along in this life
- A road map to guide me on my journey
- Water to keep me clean

I had a Bible professor who said, "What you do with the Bible will determine what God will do with you."

Ronald Reagan said, "Within the covers of the Bible are the answers for all the problems men face."

While growing up, my dad would hold up the Bible and say, "Look, kids, this is the Bible. Isn't it nice that we can hold it in our hands and read it?" This must have made a huge impression on me because as a young mother I would hold the Bible in my hands and say phrases to my little children such as, "This is the Bible," "The Bible is the Word of God," "We love the Bible." Then I would kiss it and have them do the same.

Reading the Bible has never been drudgery to me. I love to read it, and I love to study it. It truly is a wonderful treasure!

#3

Any suggestions about mothering elementary-age children?

"When I was a child…."

– 1 Corinthians 13:11

As a Child

If I were asked to describe children during their elementary years, I would say they are both very vulnerable and very impressionable. They are vulnerable because they have no control over the circumstances in their life. They live at the mercy of those who govern the situations in which they find themselves. They are also impressionable because they have a very simple trust. This simplicity makes them believe what they are told. (For example, our oldest son told our youngest daughter that she was not born into the family. He told her she was hatched from an egg, and we found her by the side of the road. She believed this until she was five years old!)

Because children are both vulnerable and impressionable, it is of the utmost importance that they be handled very carefully during these formative years—especially by their primary caregiver—their mother. How a mother interacts with her children while taking care of their physical needs will have a huge bearing on how they view themselves, those around them and the circumstances in which they find themselves both now and in the future.

For children, these are the years when they will both learn and grow. For the mother, these are years to study her children and get an understanding of what is going on in their little heads. It is a time to protect their thought processes from harmful emotions and to promote thinking patterns that will help and bless them as they grow into adulthood.

There were four areas that concerned me the most when our children were in their elementary years of childhood.

Guilt

I did not have to travel long on my parental journey to figure out that children make messes. After listening to parents older than myself, I figured out that these situations did not begin with my first child. Beverage glasses are going to be spilled on the day the floor is mopped. Cereal bowls are going to get dumped when in a hurry to get out the door. Things are going to be dropped, broken or ruined by the clumsiness or carelessness of elementary-age children. To yell, scream, lose control and say unkind things could put them on an unnecessary guilt trip. Given a

As a Child

steady diet of such reactions could scar them for a lifetime. I certainly did not want that. My dad's attitude when things went wrong was always, "As long as nobody got hurt, what difference does it make?" At least it was his attitude when the grandchildren made a mess! Messes do not have to be completely cleaned up if you are in a hurry. Broken items can be replaced, and nothing should be more precious to us than the emotional well-being of our children.

To expect elementary children to behave like mature adults is unrealistic. Children say and do things that are childish because they are *children*. They are going to act immaturely because they are immature. From time to time they will say and do things that will embarrass us. Children have a hard time sitting still; they need to have something to do. They are curious; they are going to get into things. As mothers, I believe it is important for us to understand this and help them in any way we can. We need to provide things for them to do. Things that are truly precious to us need to be placed out of harm's way.

My dad always used to say, "Kids have to grow up." And they will—in time. Until then, I do not believe a mother should put them on a guilt trip for being what they were meant to be at this time in their lives.

While in our child-bearing years, we had many well-meaning family and friends who would look for opportunities to remind us how expensive it is to rear a child. We did not need to be reminded; we were experiencing it firsthand! Visits to the doctor and dentist cost money. Christian education costs money. Participating in school activities and sports cost money. Music lessons cost money. And the list goes on and on. We chose to have six children, knowing that we would have to provide financially for all of their physical needs and beyond. We were the ones who decided if or when they needed medical care. Nothing but a Christian education for our children was ever considered. We wanted them to participate in sports and other events. We wanted them to take music lessons. Why then should we complain about how much these different activities cost us? Why should we remind them of the sacrifices we were making so that they could have or do the things that we wanted them to have or do? Why should we, as parents, burden them with guilt for being our responsibility when we wanted them to be our responsibility?

To be sure, elementary children need to be taught to be careful, to behave in a respectful manner, and to appreciate the opportunities their parents provide for them. However, as adults, we need to understand that they are still in a learning process; they will not learn these things overnight. It takes time. While they were learning, I did not want to make them feel guilty for being what they were—just children!

As a Child

Shame

As a young mother, I was well aware that there were parents who could provide nicer things for their children than we could afford to give ours. There were also those who could give their children opportunities that were far more exciting than what our children would ever be able to enjoy. This did not bother me. I would have been bothered if my children were ashamed of being who they were—ours! For this reason, I tried to put my best foot forward by...

1) Always getting them to church and school on time.

2) Making sure their school supplies were well-stocked and in good repair (i.e., lunch boxes, paper, pencils, erasers, crayons, glue, etc.).

3) Making sure they were dressed appropriately. They may not have always had department-store clothing, but I worked hard to make sure their clothing was clean and well-fitted. I did not want them to look shabby. Many thanks to my mother-in-law and sister-in-law who shopped at thrift stores and found great clothes at great prices for my elementary-age children! I will be forever grateful!

4) Always conducting myself in an appropriate manner when interacting with others. I remember as an elementary child my mother getting ready for our school programs and always trying to look nice. I remember how she interacted with our neighbors, friends, and my teachers. I was never ashamed of my mother, and I never wanted my children to be ashamed of me.

Fear

The fear of communism was very prevalent when I was an elementary child. I remember hearing the adults in my life talking about it. I remember going to church and seeing films of the persecution in communist countries. It scared me to death! It did not get much better during my teenage years. I was still scared. Then I heard a preacher say that if a person is where God wants him to be, being what God wants him to be, and doing what God wants him to do, God will always take care of him. What a relief!

The world situation today is unsteady at best. It can be frightening for a child. I never wanted my children to be burdened by fear, so I tried to assure them that God was in control and everything was going to be all right.

The financial pressures of everyday life are great. There is only so much money, and it only goes so far. When a man

As a Child

says to his wife, "We don't have any money…" she knows what he means. She knows that even though it may be tight right now, they can get through it with diligence and care. She knows that because they have honored God with their money, He will make sure that the needs of the family will be met. She immediately begins thinking of ways to ease the financial stress.

A child does not have the capacity to understand such matters. "No money" means just that—no money—no money for food, clothes, gas, house, pencils, hot lunch, McDonald's, and so on. Overhearing parents discussing finances can be very alarming. It is even worse when they hear them arguing. For this reason, I tried my best to never say to the children, "We can't afford …" or "We don't have any money." I let them buy a hot lunch at the school once a week and tried to keep a "secret stash." That way when they came to me and said, "I need new volleyball socks for P.E. tomorrow," I could go out and buy them a pair.

I do not think there is anything that can put fear in the heart of a child more than being left alone. I do not ever remember being lost from my mom or dad in a store. I can only imagine the horror that those who have experienced such a thing must have felt. I never wanted my children to feel that horror. I know there are parents who in an effort to hurry their slow-moving child out the door say things like, "If you are not in the car in five minutes, we are going to leave without you." I never could say that to my children. I never wanted them to fear that I would leave them, and they would be left all alone. I was constantly telling them, "I will never leave you on purpose. If for some reason you find yourself alone, it will not be because I left you on purpose. Just stay where you are, and when I realize you are not with me, I will come and get you." I gave more specific instructions for the different situations that might happen, but above all, I did not want them to live with the burden of this kind of fear.

Security

The famous article "Children Learn What They Live" states that if a child lives with security, he will learn to have faith. I wanted more than anything for my children to have faith in their dad and mom, their grandparents, their spiritual authorities, and, most of all, the Lord.

Being born into a pastor's family can be a little scary. To be sure, there are many wonderful people in the church who love the pastor and his family, but there are always those few who can and will make matters difficult. Along with that, offerings go up and offerings go down. People come and people go. I have been down the road of "What

As a Child

if….?" more times than I care to remember. It is not an enjoyable road to travel! Little children have big ears and love to listen in on adult conversations. These kinds of conversations can leave even an adult feeling very vulnerable and very insecure. How much more so a child!

I never wanted my children to fret about the things that were out of their control. I wanted them to know that no matter what, they would always be taken care of. I wanted them to know that I had confidence in their dad to take care of any situation and that they should have that same confidence also. Sometimes we would be in the kitchen talking, and they would bring up a situation in the church or school that would be a concern to them. I would make it a point to say, "We don't have to worry about that. That is Dad's worry, and he will take care of it." Without fail, he did, and the situation was resolved.

There were times, as well, when the children would bring up a situation concerning our own family. I considered it a great luxury to be able to say to the children, "We will tell Dad about this, and then we will do whatever he says." Sometimes I said it with confidence, sometimes with fear and trepidation. But no matter how I said it, I wanted them to know that they had an earthly father who loved them and would take care of them in any and every situation they had to face. It did not take a lot to convince them.

Answers for Emily

They had a father who was par excellence! He loved them, he cared for them, and he took great care of them. He gave them a security that led each one of them to a life of faith—not only in people, but also in the Lord. What a blessing!

Christian psychologist, Dr. Clyde Narramore, regarding mothers said, "…the marks she leaves on her children will bless or burden them for a lifetime." Truly, the years when a child is the most vulnerable and impressionable are the years when a mother needs to work the hardest to leave the mark of blessing upon her children. It does not take a lot of money, but it does take some care, some thought, and some time. It takes a mother's understanding that both her child's physical and emotional well-being are in the palms of her hands. It is up to her to make sure that the impressions that are made upon their little hearts are ones that will bless them for the rest of their lives.

"If any of you lack wisdom, let him ask of God,
that giveth to all men liberally,
and upbraideth not; and it shall be given him."
– James 1:5

#4

Is there anything you wish you had done with your kids when they were young?

"To every thing there is a season…"

– Ecclesiastes 3:1

There Is a Season

Spring, summer, fall and winter—the seasons come, and the seasons go. Each season offers its own unique opportunities of things to enjoy. It is always fun to think back over the season that has just passed and remember all the fun things that brought you pleasure. Often while reminiscing about those good times, thoughts would come such as "I wish I would have…" or "It would have been so fun if we could have…" But the season was over, so a mental note was made to put it in our plans for the next year.

Children are young only for a season. They eventually will come to an age when they are no longer little. When that season is over, it is done. There will come a time when there will not be a "next year" to do the things that were not done. Here is my list of regrets…

1) Not dating all of the pictures we took of our children when they were young.

Each time we took a picture, I thought it was such a momentous occasion that the memory would be etched in my mind forever. I had no idea that through the years that memory would get lost in the shuffle of all the other memories of the days, months, and years that had passed. If I had dated those pictures, we would not have to think so hard to determine when the event took place!

2) **Not keeping up with their baby books.**

Each child started with a baby book that I resolved I would keep up. I did a fairly good job with Hannah for about six months! I wish I would have kept a record of:

- *Visits to the doctor.* Abbie had whooping cough when she was only two years old. I would love to be able to read a written account of her symptoms, the diagnosis, prescription, recovery, how we dealt with it, etc.

- *Their firsts.* It would be nice to know when our children got their first tooth, took their first step, when I put them on the bottle, and all the other things that might be helpful to them when dealing with their own children.

- *Exciting events.* Knowing what part they had in a school or church program would be nice. Leah played the part of a flower in a school play. She did a good job, but said her part so fast that she had to gulp for air. I think she would enjoy reading about this experience as an adult.

- *Funny sayings.* Ben came up with some really good ones, but because they are not written down, we cannot remember them all.

3) Not making better birthday treats for them to take to school.

Birthdays are very special days. I feel we did a good job celebrating at home, but when it came time to sending treats to school, it was not easy. With a little thought and a little more time, I feel that I could have made their birthday celebrations at school a little more special. (Keep in mind this was pre-Pinterest!)

4) Not taking their Fall Harvest Party costumes seriously.

I do not know that I dreaded anything as much as thinking up costumes for the Fall Harvest Party! Some mothers could come up with great costumes, but I could not. They always cost me more time and more money than I wanted to spend. With a little more thought and a little more time, I could have done better. (Again, no Pinterest!)

5) Not making music lesson practice a high priority.

Music lessons cost money and time. I could have seen to it that my children practiced more. I now regret that I did not.

6) Being too lenient when it came to eating between meals and not limiting their sugar intake.

Eating between meals is not necessary and is a habit that is hard to break. Sugar is bad for the teeth and is a hindrance to controlling one's weight. I read Susanna Wesley's rules for her seventeen children way too late!

7) Not taking the time to play with them.

Our children were blessed to have a dad who spent a part of most evenings playing with them. Weather permitting, they were outside playing whiffle ball or football, bumping the volleyball, or building a snowman. When they could not be outside, they played inside. We had basketball "hoops" to shoot through, chandelier crystals to shoot at, army men to knock down with rubber bands, Memory, Caroms, Checkers, Chess, and indoor whiffle ball! They were definitely not play deprived!

When their dad was away, I considered it time to "Make hay while the sun shines!" There was so much to do, and it was so much easier to do it when my husband was away. Because of this, I did not play with the kids as much as I should have.

Looking back, I could have easily put the work aside and played with the children. Most of my children's fun memories are centered around their dad because he took the time to play with them. My not taking time to play with them is a loss that I must bear.

8) Not showing them more affection.

Although the family I grew up in was a very loving family, it was not an openly affectionate family. Not so with my husband's. I remember the first time visiting in his home and being overwhelmed by all of the hugs, kisses, and verbal expressions of love. I liked it but was not all that comfortable with it.

When the children came along, I was still struggling with it. To be sure, there was always the bedtime hug, kiss, and "I love you," but other than that, they were few and far between. Sometimes my husband would ask me if I had hugged any of the children or told them that I loved them throughout the course of the day. Most times the answer was "no." I would be ashamed and would determine to do better the next day.

I really did try. I believe all my children know their mother loved them when they were little. I believe they know I love them still today, but I wish that I had expressed it more often.

Life is busy with young children. The more children in the home, the busier it will be. I wish I had slowed down in the busyness of life to do these very simple things!

#5

Are there any family traditions you would care to suggest?

"Traditions are a valuable way to strengthen families and create lasting memories."

– Focus on the Family

Traditions

For the first ten years of our married life, we lived near my parents. It was always fun to share holidays and birthdays with my mom and dad. Every year we traveled to Atlanta to celebrate either Thanksgiving or Christmas with my husband's family. These were great times.

When in Atlanta for Thanksgiving, there was always the traditional southern cornbread dressing that was baked in a pan. If in Iowa, my mom's dressing (not cornbread) would be stuffed in the turkey. At the Anglea Christmas dinner, I always looked forward to my mother-in-law's green Christmas pear Jell-O salad with the maraschino cherry topping. When we were with my family, my mother's Christmas Jello-O was a green, red, and white layered salad. Even though I loved celebrating these special times with our respective families, I sometimes secretly wished we could (or would) begin our own family traditions.

Then the day came when we moved to Illinois. Now the birthdays and holidays were all ours to celebrate any way we wished. Now was the time to start traditions of our own.

My one goal was to make memories that the kids would look back on with fondness. Some of the things I thought were great ideas did not work. Others had to be tweaked. It was an adventure of trial and error, but eventually we came up with traditions that we were comfortable with and looked forward to as the days, months, and years flew by.

Birthdays

At least one week before each birthday, I wrapped the present and put it on display so the child would know that their birthday was not forgotten. Birthday cards that came in the mail were placed alongside the present to keep the suspense factor in play!

Each child could request the meal and type of cake they wanted for their birthday celebration. I was not really good at decorating cakes, but I did the best I could. Two books from Current, Inc., *Birthday Cakes for Kids* and *Cupcakes for Kids*, were a huge help. (This was way before the days of Pinterest!)

After the meal, we would light the candles, sing "Happy Birthday," and then they would open their cards and gifts. We tried to take our time and let them enjoy the spotlight for as long as possible.

At family devotions, we all enjoyed listening as my husband told the story of the child's birth. He would tell how we found out we were expecting, perhaps something interesting about the pregnancy, the trip to the hospital, and then how happy we both were when they were finally born.

Several years ago I came across this sweet, little poem.

The Birthday Child

Everything's been different
All the day long,
Lovely things have happened,
Nothing has gone wrong.

Nobody has scolded me,
Everyone has smiled,
Isn't it delicious
To be a birthday child?

Even though we were not always able to spend a lot of money on gifts, I made it my goal to make their birthdays truly special.

Thanksgiving

Other than the traditional Thanksgiving meal of turkey, dressing, mashed potatoes, etc., there was only one tradition that I insisted on—NO ONE IS TO COME TO

MY THANKSGIVING TABLE IN WORK CLOTHES!!! This is why…

One year it was just us. No relatives came from out of town, no one, just our family. My husband saw it as a day to catch up on some undone yard work as well as a day to play outdoors. All the while he and the children were outside working and/or playing, I was slaving away in the kitchen, trying to put on a respectable holiday meal.

When everything was set and ready, in they trooped wearing their grungy jeans/culottes and ratty-tat sweatshirts. I looked at my pretty table, all the food I had prepared, and made an announcement! From then on—no matter what, no matter where—my family would be nicely dressed for our Thanksgiving meal! (Of course, there has been many a moan and groan along the way, but I shall not be moved!)

Christmas

Christmas is truly the most wonderful time of the year at the Anglea household. We all love Christmas. The season officially starts the day after Thanksgiving. The decorations go up inside and out. Each child, spouse, and grandchild is given a Christmas list to fill out, and we, the parents, look forward to purchasing as many of the items that we can afford.

Traditions

I figured out fairly early that it is important to buy each child the same number of gifts. Younger children especially do not understand that their sister's or brother's two gifts may have cost as much as their one. They only know that sister or brother is opening one when they are not. For this reason, we set an amount of money to spend on each child and also made sure that each child had the same number of presents.

These are the things we have on the Christmas list for each child to fill out:

Name_____ (It always amused me when one of our children would include their last name!)

Books
Clothing
Accessories
Hobbies/Games/Toys
Tools (kitchen/garage/school)
Miscellaneous

We asked them to be specific with sizes, stores, etc.

We also have a stocking stuffer list that includes their favorites of the following items:

Gum	Mints	Chips/Crackers
Perfume	Aftershave	Candy Bars
Candy	Drinks	Toothpaste

Answers for Emily

Pens/Pencils	Deodorant	Magazines
Hairspray	Gift Cards	Lotion
Shampoo	Conditioner	Fast Food
	Favorite Color	

Obviously, we do not buy everything on their lists, but we keep the lists to reference for their birthdays, special gifts, etc.

For our shopping trips, I create a chart with rows that lists each of our children's names. I create columns that list the following categories: books, clothing, accessories, hobbies, tools and total. I also color coordinate these columns as follows: books—white, clothing—red, accessories—blue, hobbies—green, tools—patterns. Of course, you could adjust these columns to fit your family's needs. (See sample chart in the appendix.)

As we purchase each gift, we record it in the appropriate row and column along with the purchase price. After each shopping trip, I update the chart on the computer so it is not so messy. I do not know how we would keep our sanity if we did not use this chart.

After all the gifts are bought, then it is time to wrap.

The colors at the top of the chart are the different colors of wrapping paper I use to wrap the gifts. I wrap all of the first column's gifts in a white wrapping paper. Column two is wrapped in red, column three in blue, four in green, and

Traditions

five in whatever patterned paper I buy during the previous year's Christmas sale. When all the wrapping is done, there are five different sets of presents under our tree.

Color-coding the wrapping makes things a lot easier when it comes time to pass out the presents. We do it by round: the white round, the red round, the blue round—you get the picture, but I am getting ahead of myself.

Christmas Eve is our time to have the big family meal with appetizers, soup, games, pretty dishes, candles, punch, and, of course, the red velvet cake for dessert! It makes me teary just thinking about it. What fun!

We do not always have a "traditional" Christmas meal with ham or turkey. We just choose something that we think would make a special meal. This past year I tried to duplicate Olive Garden's chicken alfredo, breadsticks, and salad. It was delicious!

Christmas morning is either a breakfast casserole or biscuits and gravy, along with my mother's crepes with cream cheese and fruit topping.

While the kitchen gets cleaned up, the men and children rearrange the living room for the opening of presents. The Christmas story is read, a prayer is said, and then we pass out the stockings. Everyone opens them at the same time since most of the contents are the same. Once the stockings are done, it is time for the presents. We open one set (color) at a time, one person at a time, going back and forth beginning with the youngest or oldest. We take our time, but why not? It's Christmas Day, and there is no other place we would rather be than where we are—together!

Once the presents are all unwrapped and the mess is cleaned up, finger food is set out, games are played, and memories are made.

Psalm 68:6 says, *"God setteth the solitary in families...."* I am glad He did. The world is a very big place; being a part of a family unit gives us a place of belonging. Life can be uncertain. Family ties provide security. Family traditions are a wonderful reminder of who we are and where we belong. They also are a means of strengthening the ties that bind us together—one happy memory at a time!

Red Velvet Cake

½ c margarine	2 eggs
1½ c sugar	3 T cocoa
1 oz bottle of red food coloring	2¼ c flour
1 c buttermilk	¾ t salt
1 t vanilla	1 t soda
1 T vinegar	

Make paste of cocoa and food coloring. (Empty entire bottle of food coloring into cocoa and then fill bottle with water and add to paste.) Cream sugar and margarine. Add eggs and cocoa paste. Beat. Add dry ingredients and milk. Fold in vinegar and vanilla. Pour into 2 round 8-inch cake pans which have been greased and floured. Bake at 350° for 30 minutes.

Frosting

Cook 3 T flour with 1 c milk until thick. Chill until very cold.

Mix 1 c butter, 1 c sugar, 1 t vanilla. Beat for 20 minutes then combine with chilled mixture. Blend until fluffy.

Cut each cake horizontally into two layers with a serrated knife or dental floss. Frost as usual.

Crepes

1½ c flour	2 c milk
1 T sugar	2 eggs
½ t baking powder	½ t vanilla
½ t salt	2 T butter, melted

Measure flour, sugar, baking powder, and salt into bowl. Stir in remaining ingredients. Beat with a small mixer until smooth. For each crepe, lightly butter 8-inch skillet; heat over medium heat until butter is bubbly. Pour scant ¼ cup of batter into skillet; immediately rotate pan until batter covers bottom. Cook until light brown; turn and brown on other side. Spread with softened cream cheese, roll up, sprinkle with powdered sugar and top with fruit topping of choice.

# 6

Do you have any suggestions about time management with small children and a husband in the ministry?

*"So teach us to number our days,
that we may apply
our hearts unto wisdom."*

– Psalm 90:12

Never Enough Time

One day my father-in-law asked me what I considered to be the hardest thing about having six children. My answer was quick and sure. "Nothing is easy." Whatever task you would do for one, multiply it by six, and the answer is always "not easy!" No matter what you have to do, it all becomes more complicated and takes longer to accomplish with the addition of each child. Time is of the essence, and if you do not learn to use it to your advantage, it can leave you drowning in a hopeless sea of despair. Believe me, I know because I have been there! I was constantly looking for ways to make every minute count so I could get everything done that I needed to do. The following thoughts are the ones that helped me the most.

Schedule in Reverse.

Before children, it was easy to hop in the car and take off. After children, making sure everyone was dressed, had everything they needed, stayed presentable while getting into the van, and getting to our destination on time was nothing short of a miracle. While driving one day, I saw a bumper sticker that said, "Get in, sit down, shut up, and hang on!" I chuckled to myself and said, "I need one of those!" Well, I never did get one, but I did find something that eased some of the stress when trying to get from Point A to Point B with a car load of children. It was a simple two-step process of scheduling backward.

The steps are as follows:

1) Determine the time you want to arrive at Point B.

2) Working backward, schedule everything that must take place between Point A and Point B.

Because getting the kids to school was a major ordeal five days a week, I decided to tackle that particular Point A to Point B first.

Step one was easy. Since school started at 8:30 a.m., the kids needed to be at the school no later than 8:20.

Step two was a bit more complicated, but I managed to figure it out. Since it took approximately ten minutes to get to the school, we needed to be at the end of our driveway at 8:10. This meant the kids had to be in the vehicle at 8:05.

Giving them five minutes to get from the kitchen into the van meant their coats had to be on with their book bags and lunches in hand at 8:00.

Breakfast, teeth brushed, hair combed, and shoes on

should be done in thirty minutes, so they needed to be in the kitchen for breakfast by 7:30.

Allowing thirty minutes to get up, make their beds, and get dressed before coming down to breakfast meant they needed to get out of bed at 7:00.

Knowing they would not get out of bed by themselves, I determined that I should be up at 6:30 so I could make my bed, have my devotions, get them up, and get into the kitchen to have breakfast ready by 7:30.

It is important to be on time. I needed a plan, and this plan worked wonders for me. I used it all of the time, no matter where we were going. I do not remember the kids ever being late for school. I do not remember ever being late for church. Sometimes we arrived just in time, but just in time is a whole lot better than being late!

Little by Little

My pastor's wife, Mrs. Dianne Brown, taught me the value of using little blocks of time. Anything that can be done now will save you time later. For instance, it is Tuesday morning, and you are ready for ladies' soul winning. You have fifteen minutes before you must leave, and you know that when you get home you want to tackle that mountain of ironing. There is not enough time to do all of the ironing in fifteen minutes, but it is enough time to

Answers for Emily

set up the ironing board, fill the spray bottle with water, and organize the items that need to be ironed. You might even have time to choose a DVD to watch while you iron! If you are not going to iron but you know you are having baked potatoes for supper, fifteen minutes should give you enough time to count out the potatoes and wash them so they will be ready when you need to put them in the oven. "A penny saved is a penny earned," and a minute saved is just as valuable as a penny any day!

Plan your week; prioritize your days.

Not long after we were married, my mother-in-law told me how she had a certain day of the week for different household chores. She had one day to clean, one day for a quick spruce-up, one day to do laundry, and one day for grocery shopping. My mother-in-law kept a very clean and well-organized home, and I wanted to do the same. I decided that what was good for my mother-in-law was more than good enough for me.

Keeping my husband's schedule, church activities, and services in mind, I planned out my week, designating one day for the four activities mentioned above. Through the years I have had to adjust my cleaning and shopping days. As the kids got older, I found out that once a week for laundry was not enough. There were times when I had to be flexible, but for the most part, I lived and died by my weekly schedule. I found it to be a great system for getting things done and keeping the household running smoothly. (Well, at least somewhat smoothly!)

Not only did I plan my week, but I also prioritized my days. Every morning I would list what tasks needed to be done that day in the order of their importance. As each task was completed, I would run to my list and cross it off. Although not everything would always get crossed off, at least I could see that something was getting accomplished, and I was not wasting the day doing nothing.

Sometimes it is more important to save time rather than money.

Groceries are expensive. We are always looking for ways to make our grocery dollars stretch as far as possible. For a while the thought "I have more time than money" dictated my grocery choices. I was buying frozen juice concentrate to drink with breakfast. As the children grew older and started drinking larger quantities of juice, I had a hard time keeping enough made to meet their demands. The kids would grumble, and precious minutes were wasted while they waited for their juice to be prepared. Eventually I figured out that it was worth the extra dollar or two to buy their juice already prepared in a gallon jug. Many times I will sign up to provide a pasta or potato salad for a church function. I know if I run out of time, I can purchase one of these salads from GFS, put it in my own container, and no one will be the wiser!

If you need an extra hour in the day, get up an hour earlier.

Somewhere along the way, I read the autobiography of Mary Kay Ash, the founder of Mary Kay Cosmetics. I thoroughly enjoyed reading how this courageous woman founded this multi-million dollar company and how it operates still today. She was an amazing woman who is to be admired for her many accomplishments. She had many interesting and helpful things to say—one of which was that if you find you do not have enough hours in the week, get up one hour earlier each day. By simply getting up one hour earlier five days a week, you will gain five hours in which to get your work done. It sounded so simple, and it was. However, after several mornings of getting up at 5:00 a.m., I decided that maybe a good alternative would be to just work a little faster!

Do what you can and don't worry about the rest.

Nine months after moving to Bourbonnais, our fifth child was born. There were times I felt that my nose was

Never Enough Time

barely above water. Many times I knew it was just below the surface! It was March, right before the spring program, and all of us Sunday school teachers were asked to decorate our classrooms. One Sunday morning I passed one that had been decorated with the theme, "April is Bustin' Out all Over." It was incredible. Then I walked into my classroom with its pitiful excuse of a decorating job.

I was very disheartened, and I must have said something to my husband because he told me not to worry. He reminded me that I had five children to take care of and the other teachers had more time for such things than I did. I was very grateful for his advice and reminded myself that Jesus once defended a lady by saying about her, *"She hath done what she could...."* I remembered also our college president telling us students to "Do your best and hang the rest." I determined from that day forward that I would do the best I could with the time available to me and not worry about the rest. I do not want to be lazy, but I also do not want to be unreasonable!

In my Bible I keep a bookmark with this prayer on it:

Lord, I have too much to do, but it's all important.

Help me to set priorities so that I don't feel lost in the pace and the pressure.

Answers for Emily

Give me the wisdom and energy to accomplish what's necessary without wasting time or effort.

And help me make the best use of my day, remembering that time is a precious gift from You.

For years I would take that little bookmark in hand and with a sincere heart pray that exact prayer. Somehow, some way, God helped me.

Now my days are not as pressure-packed as they used to be. I look at all the mothers of young children in our church, and my heart goes out to them. I know firsthand what they are up against. Sometimes I just shake my head and ask myself, "How did I ever do it?" Looking back, I am not sure I did everything all that well, but these few, simple, tricks-of-the-trade helped tremendously. I hope they will help you too!

#7

Do you have any suggestions about life with small children and a husband in the ministry?

"And the Lord *God said,
It is not good that the man should be alone;
I will make him an help meet for him."*

– Genesis 2:18

An Help Meet for Him

One day while still a fairly young wife and mother, my dad stopped by our house. When he walked through the door, I could tell something was on his mind. He was not there two minutes before he said, "Joyce, a man cannot do it alone."

I casually nodded my head in agreement and said, "I know."

Then he told me that he had been in town helping a friend whose house was in "shambles." He shook his head as he said again, "A man just cannot do it alone." Once again, I agreed with him. He must have been doubtful that I fully understood what he was saying because a third time (and this time a little louder), he said, "A man absolutely cannot do it alone! He has to have a wife that will help him!" I am pretty sure I got it; I have not forgotten it to this day!

We all know that what my dad said is true. A man cannot do it alone. In fact, God did not intend for him to do it alone. That is why God created the woman to be the man's wife, or as He phrased it, *"an help meet for him."* A man needs a wife to help him care for himself, his home, and his children so he can take care of the work that God has called him to do. However, in order for a wife to help her husband properly, she must make sure that she is in a good enough condition to do so.

After being in the ministry for over thirty-six years, I am convinced now, more than ever, that it is important for a woman to take care of herself in the following four ways while serving in the ministry.

Physically

Every man is fully aware that when he takes his vows of "in sickness and in health" there is a possibility his wife may get so sick that he will have to take care of her. If called upon, he will honor his vows. However, that is certainly not what he wants. He wants a wife that will take care of him! I believe it is important for a wife in the ministry to take care of her health so as not to be a drag on her husband or his ministry. Here are a few commonsense suggestions for maintaining good health.

Exercise

There are various kinds of exercise equipment on which to spend your money. These are great if you can afford them, and I am sure they work well if they are used as directed. However, there is a reason why you can pick one up cheaply at a yard sale. People get bored with them, and then they want them out of their house. Believe me, I have wasted enough birthday and Christmas money on some of them to know! A much simpler solution for a busy wife and mother is walking.

For years I took a daily walk (weather permitting) down the road in front of our house. When it was too cold, windy, or hot, I walked inside with one of Leslie Sansone's "Walk at Home" DVDs. There was a one-mile walk that took about fifteen minutes and a two-mile walk that took about thirty minutes. More often than not, I did the two-mile walk. If I were really crunched for time, I did the one-mile walk. Currently I am working out on my husband's elliptical machine (he bought it, not me), but I am looking forward to warmer weather when I can get back on my bicycle for a daily six-mile bike ride.

Get Enough Sleep

Mothers of little children run tired. Oftentimes their sleep is interrupted during the night, and carrying around a little baby in those car seats must be exhausting. Taking a nap while the children are napping may be just what the doctor ordered!

Drink Lots of Water

Because your body is composed of about 60 percent water, drinking water helps maintain the balance of body fluids. Water also helps energize muscles, which means you should drink water when exercising. Drinking water helps the kidneys flush the body of toxins. Listing all of the reasons the body needs water would mean writing another book!

Take Vitamins

These do not have to be expensive. Figure out what you need, and buy what you can afford. Vitamin D is important to compensate for the lack of sunshine in the winter.

Get As Much Fresh Air as You Can.

The numerous benefits of the sun include helping us deal with stress, creating vitamin D to aid in building strong bones, fighting several types of cancers, and treating some skin conditions.

Watch Your Weight.

I have had to battle my weight all of my life. I know firsthand that it is not fun to be constantly watching what you eat. However, I have found that a person can manage her weight without too much trouble by…

- Cutting down on sugar

- Not drinking soft drinks (even diet)
- Eating steamed vegetables
- Limiting bread and potatoes
- Choosing chicken or fish over beef and pork

Being overweight causes all kinds of health problems. You will do yourself a great favor by not letting your weight get out of control. Your husband will appreciate it too!

Emotionally

When we began in the ministry over thirty years ago, I did not expect it to be a bed of roses, but I was not prepared for all the emotions I felt when it was not…

Like the day I discovered the ministry was not a money-making business…

We were newly married and just out of college when we entered the ministry. We were like every other newly married couple in our church—broke! None of us could afford anything that cost a lot of money. Then, one by one, our friends started buying newer cars, were moving into more expensive housing, and buying nicer things. I kept telling myself that someday we would be able to afford those kinds of things. Finally, one day I came to the realization that our "someday" would never come. Our friends had jobs that allowed them the freedom to "make money" while we were living on a paycheck that came from the tithes and offerings at the church.

Or when I found out that people are not always kind…

People are people. People have opinions and many are not shy about expressing those opinions. Sometimes they are not very tactful. Even the most loyal members can get sideways with the preacher, the church, the school, or someone in the church or school. They are capable of saying and doing hurtful things. When this happens, it rips your heart to shreds.

Or when church members leave the church or friends leave the ministry…

Just because someone is with you today does not mean he or she will be with you tomorrow. It is always hard to see someone leave your church—no matter what the reason. It is also hard to hear the news that someone with whom you went to college or became acquainted with in the ministry has disqualified himself, gone another direction, or just could not take it in the ministry.

Or when I realized that there is never "a day off" in the ministry…

The ministry is 24/7. No matter what, no matter where, your family is a phone call away from a change of plans.

An Help Meet for Him

These are the things I had to learn to accept as a young wife in the ministry. I knew if I did not, I would get depressed, and that would not be good for me, my husband, our children, or the ministry.

C. H. Spurgeon said, "The worst ill in the world is not poverty; the worst of ills is a depressed spirit." I found that the only cure for a depressed spirit is found in Isaiah 26:3 which says, *"Thou wilt keep him in perfect peace, whose mind is stayed on thee: because he trusteth in thee."* I believe the Lord helped me to sort it all out by bringing these thoughts to my mind-

- It is a wonderful privilege to be in the ministry. A person must be called by God to be in the ministry, and God does not call everyone. I know many people who would love to be in the ministry and would do a great job in a ministry, but God has not called them. God has called my husband, and I should consider it an honor.

- God knows our needs and will meet them according to His will. We get to have and enjoy many nice things that God has provided for us. The things we do not have, He gives us the grace to do without.

- It is only a handful of people who have issues and are unkind. The majority of the people are very considerate, loving, and kind, not only to my husband, but to me as well. Every year the ladies of our church remember me on my birthday with a very generous gift. I have much to be thankful for. Why should I let a few people ruin it for me?

- Brother Brown used to say, "Never question who God moves out of your church." We have found that disgruntled church members will cause more problems by staying than leaving.

- We are in the ministry because God called us. We cannot let what others do or not do keep us from doing what we know we are supposed to do.

- My dad used to say to me, "If you want to cry, I'll give you something real to cry about!" I do not want the Lord to give me something real to cry about.

- We all have heard the saying, "If you can't stand the heat, get out of the kitchen." Well, I cannot imagine not being in this kitchen, so I had better learn to deal with the heat!

The ministry is not always easy, but neither is it always hard. We cannot forget the many wonderful blessings we get to enjoy along the way. In order to do right by our families, we must learn to trust the Lord with the troubling circumstances of our lives. We are the ones who set the spirit in our homes.

Mentally

I remember one day in particular when I fixed pancakes for my family's breakfast. As my husband was leaving to go to the church, he kissed me goodbye and said, "Those were the best pancakes I ever put in my mouth." After he left I started to think about what he said. I thought to myself, *I have been fixing him pancakes for fifteen years, and these are the best that I've ever fixed him? You mean to tell me he has been choking down my pancakes for all these years and never told me? I wonder what else he doesn't like about me that he isn't telling me!* And my mind went off to the races! By the time he came home for supper, I was sure he was just tolerating me because leaving was out of the question. What a miserable day I spent—all because of my overactive imagination!

Women have a tendency to over-analyze, ponder, and think too much—not just about our husbands, but about life in general. We get ourselves into trouble and cause ourselves unnecessary grief by not taking the "just-the-factsma'am" approach. Life would be so much easier for us if we would do what 2 Corinthians 10:5 tells us to do when it says, *"Casting down imaginations…and bringing into captivity every thought to the obedience of Christ."*

While a teenager, I was attending a youth activity at church when my typing teacher and one of her friends walked by. I have no clue as to what they were talking about, but I do know it was an intense conversation. They stopped close enough to me that I could see my teacher point her finger at her friend and hear her say, "You are not allowed to think that way."

I am so thankful the Lord let me witness that little scene. When I can sense my thoughts getting out of control, I picture Miss Johnson pointing her finger at me and saying, "You are not allowed to think that way!" I could never even begin to count the number of times she has helped me to cast down imaginations that were not true and bring my thoughts into captivity.

Spiritually

I believe that Satan has us in his crosshairs. By "us," I mean those of us in the ministry. That he is out to destroy our families and our ministries is evident. Sometimes it seems he is doing a fairly good job. We hear far too many stories about men disqualifying themselves from the ministry because of another woman. But Satan does not give up easily. If he cannot use another woman, he will try to get to the man through his wife. Because of these tactics, we must make sure that we maintain a right relationship with the Lord. Along with daily Bible reading and prayer, it is important that we…

- **Not quench the Spirit.** 1 Thessalonians 5:19 says, *"Quench not the Spirit."* That is because the Holy Spirit was sent to give us strength and power over the devil. We hurt ourselves when we do not listen to the Holy Spirit and obey Him.

- **Keep a short account with the Lord.** A Christian does not do well with unconfessed sin in his life. Psalm 66:18 says, *"If I regard iniquity in my heart, the Lord will not hear me…."* Along with not getting our prayers answered, guilt is a horrible taskmaster. The best thing is to confess and forsake our sin as soon as we are convicted of that sin. Once our sin is confessed, we need to accept God's forgiveness and then forgive ourselves.

- **Keep our relationships right with others.** It is impossible to be right with God when we are wrong with others. Ephesians 4:32 tells us, *"And be ye kind one* *to another, tenderhearted, forgiving one another, even as God for Christ's sake hath forgiven you.*" As human beings, we are going to get our feelings hurt every now and again. It is not always easy to take wrong and forgive. But if we want God's help and blessing on our lives, we must humble ourselves, take the wrong, and forgive. If we do not, our grievance will turn into a grudge, and the grudge will lead to bitterness. Bitterness is a root that will grow and eventually defile everyone and everything we hold dear.

When traveling on an airplane, a flight attendant will take a few moments to explain the emergency procedures of the aircraft. At some point, he or she will say, "If you are traveling with a child or someone who requires assistance, secure your mask first, and then assist the other person." It does not take a rocket scientist to figure out that if the caregiver passes out, there will not be anyone available to help the one in need.

The same is true about us. Our husbands and children are depending on us to care for them and take care of their needs. We do not want to let them down. For this reason, we must take care of ourselves. Believe me, no one else can, and no one else will!

# 8

How do you plan your meals?

"…round about thy table."

– Psalm 128:3

Feed Me, I'm Yours!

It was late afternoon, and we were just about finished moving into our first apartment. My newlywed husband looked at me and asked, "What's for supper?"

My first thoughts were, *Why are you asking me? How should I know? I'll have to ask Mom!* Then it dawned on me, there was no more "Mom" to cook supper. If there was going to be food on our table, I was the one who would have to put it there. That was a very scary thought because I did not know how to cook—and I am not kidding!

Since that day, it has been a very eventful journey of getting food on the table. I started this journey with a very "Que Sera, Sera, whatever will be, will be" attitude. Figuring out that this train of thought was not going to work did not take long. After watching my husband shake his head as he looked at the food I placed before him and hearing him sadly say, "I don't remember my mother ever ruining an entire meal," I decided it was time to get serious about our mealtimes.

I studied my cookbooks like I was studying for a college

exam. Every time I heard my husband compliment a cook, I asked for the recipe. I made it a matter of prayer and earnestly asked the Lord for divine wisdom, help, mercy, and grace. Looking back over my multitude of messes and many failures, I am reminded of the words, "Through many dangers, toils, and snares, I have already come…" and I *really* am not kidding!!!

Along with not knowing how to cook, I was stumped by what to cook and when to cook it. I badly needed help and sought advice from anyone whom I felt worthy. It was my mother-in-law who helped me the most when she said that she never fixed the same meat two nights in a row. I figured if she did not do it, neither should I, and so I began by scheduling my evening meals as follows:

Monday:	Chicken
Tuesday:	Ground meat (this included lasagna, spaghetti, anything using ground meat)
Wednesday:	Casserole
Thursday:	Beef, Fish, Pork
Friday:	Chili (winter); Grilled hamburgers (summer)
Saturday:	Homemade Pizza
Sunday:	Soup/Sandwich (winter); Salad/Sandwich (summer)

Feed Me; I'm Yours!

When planning these meals, I took the advice from my good friend, Cindy Hall, who said she prepared only four things for every evening meal: a meat, starch, vegetable, and salad. I figured if it was good enough for her family, it was good enough for mine. I follow her example still today.

Because a schedule worked so well for the evening meals, I decided to try it for our breakfast meals, also. Our breakfast schedule went like this:

Monday: Pancakes, Waffles, French toast—anything that had to be topped with syrup
Tuesday: Breakfast Casseroles
Wednesday: Chipped Beef on Toast, Lil' Smokies wrapped in crescent rolls, Egg and Cheese Sandwiches, or Biscuits and Gravy. (No, I did not make homemade biscuits.)
Thursday: Cold cereal (The kids never liked oatmeal.)
Friday: Fried eggs made by dad!
Saturday: Whatever they could find or breakfast leftovers. (Once they were old enough, they were on their own—happy day!)
Sunday: Muffins, Cinnamon rolls, or Coffeecake

This menu took care of the morning and evening meals, but I was stumped by what to have for lunch. I decided

Answers for Emily

to make it easy; lunch would always be a sandwich, chips, and a cookie for dessert—all served on a paper plate! *Voilà! Perfecto!* A touch of genius!

Because my family has always wanted something sweet after the evening meal, I have always made at least one dessert a week. Also, there must be ice cream and chocolate syrup always, always, always in the freezer and refrigerator. We cannot live without our ice cream! (At least we do not live as happily without our ice cream!)

The day before my designated grocery shopping day, I would make up a menu according to my schedule. Then I would gather all of the recipes I would be using and made a grocery list according to the items needed. When I realized that I was using many of the same recipes over and over, I purchased a recipe box, copied the recipes on 3x5 cards, and filed them accordingly. It saved me a lot of time and hassle!

Around the time our first child was born, a book became popular among young mothers called *Feed Me, I'm Yours* by Vicki Lansky. This book was written to help mothers feed their toddler children with healthy, homemade baby food. I read it and found some of what was written helpful, but it was the title that really stuck with me. There were many times when I would look at my family and

Feed Me; I'm Yours!

imagine them looking at me with eyes that were pleading, "Feed me, I'm yours." This general schedule helped to make the meal planning, grocery shopping, and preparation so much easier-and that is exactly what I needed to keep my very food-conscious brood at least somewhat happy.

When our oldest daughter Hannah got married, I made her a cookbook and titled it *Keeping in the Kitchen*. It was a compilation of most of the recipes in my recipe box that I had used during her growing up years. She loved it and still uses it today. Each new Anglea bride has been (or will be) presented with her own edition of our family cookbook. In the front of each book is this little note:

To be a successful "keeper at home" one must spend much time in the kitchen. Planning and preparing meals takes much time and effort, but it is worth every minute when it is evident your family is enjoying their time around the table.

It is my hope and prayer that this collection of our favorite recipes, as well as the hints from family and friends, will be a blessing to you as you become the keeper of your own home.

Meal time is an important time because it is the time when a family gathers together as one unit. It should be a time when the cares and stresses of the day can be put aside and each member of the family can relax and enjoy being in each other's company. When a wife and mother takes the time to prepare food that she knows her family will enjoy, she makes it all possible! I always picture the family of the Proverbs 31 woman sitting around the table when they rise up and call her blessed!

#9

Any tips on rearing boys?

*"…the prophecy
that his mother taught him."*

– Proverbs 31:1

Boys Will Be Boys

We have all heard it said that there is a special relationship between a mother and her sons. Any woman who has ever had a son knows this is true. However, do not let it fool you; there is a special bond between a man and his sons.

I will never forget when our first son, Ben, was born. Back then we did not have all the technology available today. We had no way of knowing what our unborn baby would be. As soon as the nurse (or doctor, I can't remember which!) said, "It's a boy!" my husband became elated. He walked around the room saying, "A boy! A boy! I got me a boy!" Then he came over to me and with tears in his eyes said, "Thank you for giving me a boy!" (Like I had anything to do with it!!) He started walking around the room again, and I heard him say again, "A boy, a boy, I got me a boy!"

That was my very first clue as to how a man feels about having a son. Six years later our second son, Luke, was born. Again, no ultrasound, and again, when it was announced that we had a boy, my husband walked around the room saying, "A boy! A boy! I got me another boy!" Then to me, "Thank you for giving me another boy!" (Don't tell me there isn't a special bond between a man and his sons!)

I must admit, after having a girl first, I was not all that sure what to do with a boy. This was definitely new and uncharted territory. But I had heard enough, seen enough and read enough to know there were some things I absolutely, positively did not want for my sons. They were as follows:

I did not want my sons to be "mama's boys."

I had heard several sermons where the preacher mentioned mothers who kept their married children attached to their apron strings. They warned about the children not being able to do anything without checking with Mama first. I did not want that for any of my children. I especially did not want that for my sons. I wanted my boys to be known as their father's sons—not "Mama's little boys."

I did not want to ruin the whole "male-bonding" thing.

One evening when Ben was just a little guy, Hannah and I went to some sort of ladies' get together at the church. This left dad and son home alone for a couple of hours. When Hannah and I arrived back at the house, the two of them had this "I-got-caught-with-my-hand-in-the-cookie-jar" expression on their faces. When we asked them what they had done all evening, Ben looked at his dad (as

Boys Will Be Boys

if asking for permission), and then, almost whispering, said, "We wrestled with our shirts off!" No girls were in the house, and they had wrestled with their shirts off! What I witnessed that evening was priceless. I realized this was a definite "guy thing," and I did not want to do anything to ruin it. I only wanted to fan it and keep it alive and well!

I did not want to ever connive with my sons against their father.

I believe one of the saddest commentaries on a mother/son relationship was Rebekah's pitting her son Jacob against his father Isaac. I never, ever wanted to do that with my sons.

Just as sure as there were things I did not want, there were some qualities I desperately wanted to see exhibited in each of their lives. I knew my husband wanted these qualities for them as well, so I tried to help bring them about by doing what I could. They are as follows:

To know how to make decisions

As soon as they were old enough, I let them pick out what they were going to wear.

When they were still very little and needed help getting dressed, I chose two different outfits, laid them out in front of them and said, "Which one would you like to wear?"

It was a simple thing, but I thought it might help them to learn how to make decisions. I was constantly looking for similar situations where they could make their own choices, and then I let them do it.

To have manly characteristics

Years ago I saw an advertisement for a perfume that said, "Want him to be more of a man? Try being more of a woman." I can still see those words in my mind's eye. I have tried to work it with my husband, and I tried to work it with my boys. I did the usual things like having them open jars and as soon as they were able, I had them pump the gas, etc.

Then one day I heard a teacher say that women should never *tell* a man what she wants him to do, she should *ask* him to do what she wants him to do. I immediately thought of my boys and decided that I was going to change my approach when needing them to get things done. For instance, instead of saying, "Luke, go take out the trash," I said, "Luke, would you take out the trash for me?"

I was amazed at the difference in the reaction I received! It became my new "weapon of warfare," and the battles I won were well worth all of the effort of reworking my thought process. Now, lest you think everything was "Polly Perfect" from there on out, there were times when they returned

Boys Will Be Boys

home from school that I would meet them at the door and say, "You will go straight to your room, you will make your bed, you will hang up your clean clothes and put your dirty ones down the chute before you even think of doing anything else!" But those times were very few and far between!

To have good manners

I tried like everything to make sure they had good table manners. I knew that someday they would be on a date with some special girl, and they would want to make sure they were doing things just right. So every now and again, I would go over how to seat a girl at the table and what eating utensil to use when. One thing I never wanted to tolerate was hearing them make body noises (of any kind) while at the table. If I would have had my way, they would have been excused from the table immediately. However, all I could get away with was a stern, verbal reprimand or giving them a look that could have killed them in an instant. At least I always received an "Oh, excuse me," which was hardly enough, but it was better than nothing!

To be able to handle the responsibility of a family

I tried to take advantage of times when my husband was out of town to instill in them the responsibility of caring for a family. On these occasions as soon they were old enough,

Answers for Emily

I would ask them to check and make sure the garage door was down, and the doors to the outside were closed and locked. The oldest son was allowed to sit in Dad's chair at the table for supper and lead in family devotions at night. When they earned their driving permits, I had them drive me to and from church. I never told them how to drive unless I felt that my life or my car were in danger!

To be able to leave his father and his mother and cleave to his wife

From the first time I laid my eyes on our sons until the day they were married, I kept in mind that I was not rearing them for myself; I was rearing them for another woman. Above all, I wanted that woman to be happy with me. I tried my best to love them and to take care of them without dominating them. I wanted it to be easy for them to leave our home and to make their wives the most important person in their lives. I have never wanted to come between either of my sons and their wives—I may have to live with one of them someday!

I heard my dad say many times that little boys always must be doing something. I never doubted him, but I never really believed him until I had one of my own. Then I found out it was true. While some of the things they had to be doing caused frustration, there were other things that absolutely melted my heart! I also found out that little boys do not stay little forever. As they grew, they began doing things that brought me much joy and happiness. Those things made all the frustration of the earlier years well worth it.

I love my boys. There is indeed a special bond between a mother and her sons. I am so glad that the Lord has allowed me the privilege of having two such relationships!

#10

Any tips on rearing girls?

*"…As is the mother,
so is her daughter."*

– Ezekiel 16:44

Sugar and Spice and Everything Nice

As happy as my husband was to have a boy, that is how happy I was to have a girl! Every time I heard the words, "It's a girl!" my heart said a great big "YES!" I smiled every time! What an adventure! What a joy! I knew exactly where she was coming from, what she was thinking and where she was headed. There was no wondering; it was all knowing. Sometimes it was frustrating, but even in the midst of the frustration, it was great! I love having girls!!!

Just like with the boys, there were some things that I definitely did not want for any one of my girls. My biggest concern was that they not be…

Mean and Catty

I grew up reading the *Little House on the Prairie* books by Laura Ingalls Wilder. Laura's school friends were as familiar to me as the children in my own classroom. Every time I looked into the face of one of our newborn baby girls, I knew I did not want that little girl to be a Nelly Olson. I tried hard to instill in each of them the importance of being kind to every one—even when the person was less than lovely or was acting in an obnoxious manner.

I also did not want them to be…

Loud and Silly

I had seen enough girls acting so loud and so silly that I knew that was not how I wanted any daughter of mine to behave (especially when they were in the company of boys). Loud and silly is not respectful. Loud and silly is odious and shameful. I wanted my girls to behave appropriately in every situation—whether at church, a youth activity, ball game—whatever. I did not want them to be wallflowers; I wanted them to participate and have a good time, but I wanted them to do it without clamoring for attention.

As much as I did not want them to be mean and catty or loud and silly, I wanted them to be…

Comfortable in Their Clothes

I knew they were going to be dressed differently than other girls when we went to town, the playground, or anywhere other than church. I wanted them to be comfortable wearing their culottes and modest dresses. Because of this desire, I tried my best to make them cute culotte outfits that fit them well. Since I sewed most of their dresses and skirts, I could add extra length or raise a neckline without the garment looking "fixed." While shopping, if I found a dress or skirt that was perfectly modest, I bought it or made them one that looked similar.

A time comes in a girl's life when she becomes aware of what others are wearing. It is not always easy for a girl when she realizes that other girls look good in clothing that she is not allowed to wear. I worked hard to dress my girls so they would be comfortable and not feel self-conscious about what they were wearing.

Another item on the top of my list was that they be…

Feminine

It did not take long to discover that each of our four girls had their own unique style. Some of the girls gravitated toward feminine things more than the others, but my goal was that not one of them would grow up looking or acting like a man. I tried to be a good example, pointed out the feminine traits of others, and praised them for anything they did that was femininely noteworthy. Three of the four were easy, but there was one who simply did not want to go along with the program. We had several, (and I mean several) ruined Sunday mornings because of her not wanting to wear lacy socks to church! After a while I decided it was far more important to go to church peacefully than to demand she dress according to my definition of femininity. Thankfully she has grown up to be a lovely, feminine young woman. She may not be all ribbons and lace, but at least she is not wearing combat boots!

Another thing I wanted for my girls was for them to be able to...

Handle Their Emotions

I knew my girls were going to be emotional. I am emotional. Every woman I know is emotional. We are not emotional because we are weak; we are emotional because it is how God made us. To fight against being emotional is to fight against God's divine purpose and design. However, to let our emotions get out of control is unacceptable. It can even be dangerous to one's health.

Whether they were on top of the world or in the depths of despair, I wanted them to be able to handle the situation without making a spectacle of themselves or making life miserable for those around them. My ultimate goal for getting them to handle their emotions as children and teenagers was that they be able to handle what would come their way as adult women. I did not want them to make their husband's life miserable because they were emotionally unstable. I do not know who coined the phrase "Just deal with it," but that person was right on target. There is always something for a woman to deal with!

I wanted them to be prepared for the…

Changes in Their Bodies

One of the most exciting times in the life of a young girl is when she becomes aware that her body is changing. It can also be a bit scary. I did not have any older sisters to pave the way for me, and for some reason, my mother was not comfortable talking with me about this matter. It was a very awkward time for both of us. I did not want that for my daughters. I watched them closely. When I saw their bodies beginning to develop, I tried to make sure they knew I was aware of what was happening. I wanted them to know I was ready to help them during this transition time from little girl to young woman. When they needed more substantial undergarments, we went together to get them. I explained to them about menstrual cycles and kept products on hand so they would have them when the big day came. I also talked with their school teachers so that if anything happened while at school, they would have what they needed, when they needed it. All four of my girls have been a bit anemic. Because of this, they needed to take women's

One-A-Day vitamins. These gave them the extra iron they needed to get them through their time of the month without being totally wiped out.

Some things I found out about rearing little girls…

The Combing Challenge

It did not matter how slowly and carefully I combed, they always complained that I was hurting their heads. They would squirm and move their heads, which made it even harder.

I tried everything. I tried being gentle. I tried conditioners and spray-on products. I tried anything and everything that promised to make this task not so difficult.

Finally, I just said, "Yes, I know it hurts. It hurt when my mom combed my hair. It's just the way it is. Just sit still, and I'll be done in a minute." All I can say is it was a very happy day when they were able to comb their hair for themselves!

Two's Company, Three's a Crowd

Girls are not only emotional, they are relational. Whenever there are three girls in a close friend relationship—watch out!—because there is always one who feels left out. I observed this during my younger sister's growing up years, and I saw it with our oldest daughter during her grade school and high school years. It was not fun. Some days she would come home all smiles, and I knew she had not been the one on the outside looking in. Other days it was obvious that she was the one who had been left out. We had many talks. Many times, I would tell her what my mom told me, "If they don't want to be your friend, go find someone who does." I also reminded her that "In order to have a friend, you have to be one."

Another Woman in the House

By the time each girl's senior year rolled around, she was well on her way to becoming her own woman. She had ideas of her own, and she was figuring out that there were other ways to do things besides the way Mom did them. This was fine with me, until she got in my way. Then I had to bite my tongue.

After each girl's senior year was complete, it was time to get her ready for college. My husband took his part of this task very seriously. He spent much time talking with each girl about her car, bank account, etc. I am ashamed to say there were times when I felt the slightest twinge of jealousy as I watched my husband talking to this little girl who had somehow grown up to become "another woman in the house." It is not always easy to share your husband with another woman, even when she is your own flesh and blood.

Answers for Emily

∼

When a daughter is married, she is given away to become another man's wife. It is not easy for a dad to give away his daughter. I remember the look on my dad's face as he walked me down the aisle! He looked positively mournful. A mother may not mourn, but it is not easy for her either. However, I discovered an unexpected blessing. Once she is given away, an avenue is opened for her to become your very closest friend. In my opinion, that is the best part of rearing girls!

#11

Any school-related routines that worked well for your family that you think might help mine?

"And Jesus increased in wisdom…."

– Luke 2:52

Readin' and 'Ritin' and 'Rithmetic

School was taken very seriously in the Anglea household. My husband has always said, "You only get one shot to educate your children." He was determined that our children would receive the best education possible. Most (if not all) of our school-related routines were his doing, and he was adamant that they be adhered to. There were times when I thought he was being a bit overboard. Now that five of our six children have successfully graduated from college, I am very glad he was so insistent when I would have let some things go.

These were the areas he felt were important…

An Early Bedtime

This was not always easy, especially on Wednesday nights or during special meetings. However, he never wanted me to linger long at the church. He wanted me to get the kids home and ready for bed so they would get as much sleep as possible. When they were in kindergarten or the early grade school years, 8:00 p.m. was their bedtime. For high school, it was 10:00 p.m. Needless to say, our children never went to school bragging about how late their parents let them stay up the night before. I think they were somewhat embarrassed about how early they had to go to bed.

Homework Packets

At our school on every Tuesday, a homework packet is sent home with each student with all of his or her schoolwork from the previous week in it. The parents are to look at their child's work, sign the packet, and return it the next day.

All I had to do was glance at the contents; my husband went over every paper with a magnifying glass! He wanted to see exactly what was going on. He would not hesitate to question the children or their teacher when he felt it was necessary. He was much like a bulldog when it came to our children's grades. I must say, it paid off. I do not remember any of them not being on the honor roll. There may have been a few, brief times when they were on the "B" honor roll, but for the most part, it was always the "A" honor roll. This was to my husband's credit, not mine.

Readin' and 'Ritin' and 'Rithmetic

Breakfast Every Morning

My husband is a breakfast eater; I could not care less if I eat in the morning, but I woke up every morning and made sure the kids had something more than donuts and Pop-tarts in their stomachs before they left for school. I believe my diligence paid off. Studies show that breakfast is the most important meal of the day for kids. I do know it is hard to concentrate on any empty stomach, and if you have a hard time concentrating, it is not easy to learn.

The areas I concentrated on were these…

Decent Lunches

For a while, we (my husband packed more than his fair share) were packing five lunches a day. At times it was a real challenge. I bought the best lunch meat I could afford for their sandwiches and made sure they had a nice treat to enjoy.

Of course, they all wanted cute lunch boxes, and I tried to save money by using reusable plastic containers. But one day I decided I had put up with all the mold I could handle and decided that brown paper bags and Ziploc baggies were the way we were going to go. (And I didn't feel one bit bad about all the money I wasted by doing so!)

Answers for Emily

Buying School Supplies

To make things easier in August, I began buying their next year's school supplies in June. One week I would buy all of their crayons; the next, pencils; the next, glue sticks; etc. I was so happy to tell my husband that everything, except for their book bags, had already been purchased when it came time for school to start in the fall.

Cookie and Brownie Mixes

There were a lot of cookies and brownies to be made during the school year. I had to come up with a way to make the whole baking process as simple as possible. We would go to Sam's Club and buy baking ingredients in bulk. Then I would take my favorite cookie and brownie recipes, measure out the sugar ingredients and put them in Ziploc bags. Then I would do the same with the flour, baking powder, etc. If there were chocolate chips or other add-ins, I would measure them out and put them in bags as well. I would label each bag and put them in the freezer. When I needed to bake, all I had to get out were the two or three Ziploc bags, eggs, butter/oil and vanilla. The plan worked great!

Readin' and 'Ritin' and 'Rithmetic

Participation

School is not just about the time spent in the classroom. There are lots of extra-curricular activities like sports, music programs, mission and science projects, and spirit weeks. My husband made sure we were at every home game and out-of-town game or tournament to which we could reasonably drive.

I, on the other hand, did my best to make sure they had all of the materials, costumes, or whatever was needed for their projects or events. It did get a bit overwhelming at times, but I never wanted to squelch their excitement or enthusiasm. It always made me happy when they were happy with their degree of participation.

∽

School is a have-to. Children must go to school. Once their school days are over, it is over. There is no going back. What has been learned is learned, and what has not been learned is left behind. I do not regret any effort we made to enhance our children's education. It was all very worth it.

#12

If you could write a list of "Hints & Tips for the Housewife," what would some of them be?

"Every wise woman buildeth her house..."
(with a little help from her friends!)

"Every Wise Woman Buildeth Her House..."

Most young women begin their house-building careers with very little experience or knowledge. At least I think they do. I know I did! Compared to all that is involved in house-building, my experience was almost nil, and my knowledge was limited to how my mother did it. It did not take long to figure out that what worked so well for my mom did not guarantee it would work easily for me. I needed help, and I needed it badly!

I began reading and studying women's magazines. I began asking advice from any woman (young or old) who looked like she might know something about anything in the whole home-building process. At family gatherings, I would pick the brains of my grandmother, mother, mother-in-law, sister, sisters-in-law, aunts, or cousins. At church, I would question my co-workers in the nursery, my partner out soul winning, or the one I was sitting next to during choir practice. From all these women I gained many valuable tips, hints, and advice. The following are the ones I have used the most over the years:

Cleaning Tips

The earlier in the week you clean your house, the longer it will stay clean.

Keep your house picked up; even if it is not clean, it will look like it.

This window cleaner came from my mother-in-law, and I've used it for years.

> ⅛ c ammonia (not lemon)
> ½ c rubbing alcohol
> ⅛ c white vinegar
> Water to make one quart

Always wear tennis shoes when working in your house. It will help you work faster and more efficiently.

The empty look is the clean look.

Cooking Tips

Burned food in pans? Sprinkle several tablespoons of baking soda in the pan with a little warm water and simmer. I promise you this tip really works!

Awful smell from burned food? Pour one teaspoon of vanilla in a pan of water and boil on the stove. No one will ever know!

When preparing dishes to be refrigerated and baked later, write the baking directions on a piece of paper or sticker that can be put on the cover of the baking dish. This way you can put away your cookbook and will not have to get it out when it is time to bake the food.

Keep a place to store recipes you run across and would like to try "someday." Then when you are tired of fixing the same old dishes or do not know what to fix, pull out these recipes and try something new!

Whenever possible, to help make the cleanup go faster, prepare your food in the dish in which you will serve it.

Before starting a recipe, put all of the ingredients and supplies on the counter. As you use each item, put away the ingredient and load any dirty bowls/utensils in the dishwasher. When you are ready to put the dish in the oven or refrigerator, the counter is clear, and you know you have not left anything out of the recipe.

When making mashed potatoes, warm the milk in the microwave first. This will ensure hot mashed potatoes when they reach the table.

Baking Tips

When making bar cookies such as marshmallow treats, use waxed paper to press the mixture into the pan.

For a softer cookie, bake the minimum amount of minutes and remove them just before they look done. They will get firmer as they cool.

Chill cakes in the refrigerator before icing for easier spreading of frosting.

When peeling apples for pie, place the sliced apples in salt water. This will prevent the apples from turning brown.

Always keep a bottle of Vitamin E oil near your stove. If applied immediately when burned, it will keep the burn from blistering.

This and That

Vinegar can be used instead of expensive liquid fabric softener or dryer sheets.

Store items in square containers rather than round. The square containers utilize all possible space, whereas the round containers lose the "corner" space between containers.

Clothespins work great for closing opened bags of chips and hanging skirts on wire hangers.

To keep your drains clog-free, once a week pour ½ cup baking soda and 1 cup white vinegar down the drain. Let stand a few minutes and then flush with hot water.

Make your bed as soon as you get up in the morning so you will not have to make it before you go to bed at night.

To help prevent colds, flu, and illnesses, use a clean dishcloth each time you do dishes.

Do not be too proud to ask your mother-in-law for advice!

Favorite Quotes

"You make your husband happy; let God make him holy." – Joy Rice Martin

"It is better to go through life wanting what you don't have than having what you don't want." – Dianne Brown

"It is nice to be important, but it's more important to be nice." – John Templeton

"Today is the tomorrow you worried about yesterday and all is well." – Unknown

Answers for Emily

"Let the wife make the husband glad to come home and let him make her sorry to see him leave." – Martin Luther

And my most favorite of all...
"Home is the nicest word there is."
– Laura Ingalls Wilder

~

Several years ago at Christmastime, Jewel-Osco had a radio advertisement that was a take on the nursery rhyme "This is the house that Jack built." It was one of the cutest, catchiest radio clips I have ever heard. I wish I could recall the whole sequence, but I know it ended with "...all in the home that she built." When I heard those last seven words, with the emphasis on the word "she," I gulped as I envisioned a sign over the door into our kitchen saying, "This Is the Home that Joyce Built."

I thought to myself, *I hope I have built a nice home for my family.*

I do not claim to have all the answers when it comes to house-building; that is why I am still comparing notes with other ladies today. But I can say that through the years I have worked very hard *trying* to build my house into a well-organized, happy home—a home where every member of my family will be comfortable when in it and will be eager to get back to when away. If I have obtained any measure of success, it is not because I am so smart; it is because I had a lot of help from my friends!

Dear Reader,

Now that you have read my answers to Emily's questions, there is one question I would like to ask you. *Do you know for sure that you will spend eternity in heaven?* If not, please let me share with you how you can know this from the Word of God in four simple steps:

Step One: You must realize that you are a sinner. Romans 3:23, "For all have sinned and come short of the glory of God."

While it is true that we sin every day, this is not what makes us a sinner. We are sinners not because of what we do but because of who we are. We are human beings who are born with a sin nature. When Adam and Eve were created, they were created as perfect human beings. They chose to disobey God, and when they did, the entire human race was tainted with sin. We cannot help ourselves; we are sinners by birth. God is perfect, and we fall short of His glory.

Step Two: You must realize that there is a price that must be paid for sin. Romans 5:12, "…and so death passed upon all men, for that all have sinned." Romans 6:23, "For the wages of sin is death.…"

The payment for our sin is death; this death is not a physical death but a spiritual death. It is death in that awful place called hell. Heaven is a perfect place. No sin is allowed in heaven. We cannot go to heaven in our sinful condition.

Now here is another question: do you think God wants you to pay for your sin by spending eternity in hell? The obvious answer is "No, of course not!" God created you and loves you. He wants you to spend eternity in heaven with Him. He made a way for you to be able to go to heaven. What did He do? It is found here in the next step.

Step Three: You must realize that Jesus died on the cross to pay the price for your sin. Romans 5:8, "But God commendeth his love toward us, in that, while we were yet sinners, *Christ died for us.*"

God sent Jesus down to earth as a tiny baby. We celebrate His birth at Christmas. But Jesus did not stay a tiny baby. He grew up, and at the age of 33, He died on the cross to pay the wages of death for our sin.

Romans 6:23 "…but the *gift* of God is eternal life *[heaven]* through Jesus Christ our Lord."

Just because Jesus died on the cross does not mean

that everybody will go to heaven, but it does mean that everybody can. The key word is *gift*. A gift is purchased for somebody. A gift is offered to somebody. However, it is up to that somebody to accept or reject the gift. Salvation has been purchased for you by the blood that Jesus shed when He died on the cross. It is offered to you today. It is up to you to accept or reject this gift.

Step Four: You must put your faith and trust in Jesus alone to take you to heaven. Romans 10:9, "That if thou shalt confess with thy mouth the Lord Jesus, and shalt believe in thine heart that God hath raised him from the dead, thou shalt be saved." Romans 10:13, "For whosever shall call upon the name of the Lord shall be saved."

The only way a person can be saved from eternal death in hell is to admit that he or she is a sinner, know that one cannot do anything to save oneself, and trust the death, burial and resurrection of Jesus Christ to pay for the debt of his or her sins.

Every person who trusts in Jesus Christ alone for the payment of his or her sins will escape eternal separation from God and enjoy everlasting life with Him in heaven.

"For God so loved the world that He gave His only begotten Son that whosoever believeth in him should not perish but have everlasting life" (John 3:16).

Answers for Emily

If you would like to accept this gift of salvation, here is a simple prayer to guide you:

Dear Lord Jesus,
　　I know I am a sinner. I know that because of my sin I deserve to spend eternity in hell. I believe that You died on the cross and rose from the dead to save me. I trust You now to be my Savior. Please come into my heart, forgive me for my sins and take me to heaven when I die. In Jesus' name, Amen

Thank you for reading this last answer. I pray if you have not already trusted Jesus to be your Savior, you will do so today.

　　　　　　　　　　　　　With kindest regards,

　　　　　　　　　　　　　Joyce Anglea

　　　　　　　　　　　　　Joyce Anglea

	White–Books	Red–Clothing	Blue–Accessories	Green–Hobbies	Pattern–Tools	Total
Hannah						
Jason						
Ben						
Ashley						
Abbie						
Alan						
Luke						
Jessica						
Leah						
Peter						
Cherith						